W9-AAR-302

GRILL EATS & DRINKS

RECIPES FOR GOOD TIMES

CHRONICLE BOOKS
SAN FRANCISCO

Material on pages 6–9, 12–15, 48–57, and 62–63 previously published in *Picnics*
by Sara Dressen (text copyright © 2004 by Chronicle Books LLC and photographs
copyright ©2004 by Jonelle Weaver) by Chronicle Books LLC.

Material on pages 10–11, 16–19, and 28–29 previously published in *The Seriously Simple Deck*
(text copyright © 2002 by Diane Rossen Worthington and photographs copyright © 2000
by Maura McEvoy) by Chronicle Books LLC.

Material on pages 20–27, 30–37, 40–43, and 46–47 previously published in
Dad's Awesome Grilling Book (text copyright © 2009 by Bob Sloan and photographs
copyright © 2009 by Antonis Achilleos) by Chronicle Books LLC.

Material on pages 38–39 and 44–45 previously published in *Seriously Simple* (text
copyright © 2002 by Diane Rossen Worthington and photographs copyright © 2002
by Noel Barnhurst) by Chronicle Books LLC.

Material on pages 58–61 previously published in *Tropical Cocktails Deck*
(text and photographs copyright © 2008 by Mittie Hellmich) by Chronicle Books LLC.

Library of Congress Cataloging-in-Publication Data available.

ISBN 978-1-4521-4117-6

Manufactured in China

MIX
Paper from
responsible sources
FSC™ C008047
FSC
www.fsc.org

Design by Vanessa Dina

10 9 8 7 6 5 4 3 2 1

Chronicle Books LLC
680 Second Street
San Francisco, California 94107
www.chroniclebooks.com

CONTENTS

▼▼▼▼▼

QUICK-PICKLED VEGGIES

2 cups [200 g] small cauliflower florets

2 cups [200 g] ½-in- [12-mm-] thick small zucchini slices

1 cup [90 g] 1-in [2.5-cm] green bell pepper squares

1 cup [90 g] 1-in [2.5-cm] red bell pepper squares

2 sprigs fresh tarragon

2½ cups [600 ml] water

1½ cups [360 ml] white wine vinegar

¾ cup [180 ml] unseasoned rice vinegar

⅔ cup [130 g] sugar

One 2½-in [6-cm] piece fresh ginger, peeled and cut into thin slices

7 garlic cloves, peeled and halved

1 Tbsp kosher salt

2 tsp yellow mustard seeds

1½ tsp red pepper flakes

Combine the cauliflower, zucchini, bell peppers, and tarragon in a large, nonreactive bowl or wide-mouthed jar and set aside. Bring the water, wine vinegar, rice vinegar, sugar, ginger, garlic, salt, mustard seeds, and red pepper flakes to a boil in a large pot. Lower the heat to a simmer and cook for 10 minutes. Bring to a boil again and pour the hot liquid over the vegetables. Stir occasionally while the mixture cools, then cover and refrigerate. Wait at least 3 days before eating, stirring every once in a while to keep all of the vegetables submerged. When serving, make sure to avoid the ginger and garlic, which are for flavoring, not eating. The pickles keep in the refrigerator for up to 1 week.

SERVES 6 TO 8

MARINATED OLIVES

2 cups [400 g] unpitted olives, a mixture of both green and black, such as picholine, niçoise, and Kalamata, large and small

2 Tbsp olive oil

6 thin strips of lemon peel, ¼ tsp finely chopped lemon zest, plus 1 tsp freshly squeezed lemon juice

6 thin strips of orange peel, plus ¼ tsp finely chopped orange zest

2 garlic cloves, cut into thin slices

¼ tsp whole coriander seeds

1 bay leaf

Combine all the ingredients in a medium bowl, cover, and marinate in the refrigerator for at least 2 days, stirring occasionally. Serve or store covered in the refrigerator for up to 1 week.

SERVES 6

SUMMER VEGETABLE GUACAMOLE SALSA

2 large tomatoes, peeled, seeded, and finely diced

½ red bell pepper, seeded and diced

½ yellow bell pepper, seeded and diced

1 large carrot, peeled and diced

1 ear fresh corn, kernels cut from the cob

2 Tbsp finely chopped fresh cilantro, plus cilantro leaves for garnish

2 Tbsp finely chopped fresh flat-leaf parsley

1 jalapeño chile, seeded and finely chopped

2 Tbsp fresh lemon juice

Kosher salt and freshly ground black pepper

1 avocado, peeled, pitted, and cut into ½-in [12-mm] pieces

Tortilla chips

In a medium bowl, stir together the tomatoes, bell peppers, carrot, corn kernels, chopped cilantro, parsley, jalapeño, and lemon juice. Season with salt and pepper. Cover and refrigerate for up to 1 hour.

Spoon the salsa into a serving bowl. Gently stir in the avocado. Taste and adjust the seasonings. Garnish with cilantro leaves and serve with tortilla chips.

MAKES ABOUT 1 QT [900 G]

CURRIED DEVILED EGGS

12 large eggs, at room temperature

⅔ cup [150 g] mayonnaise

2 Tbsp freshly squeezed lemon juice

1½ tsp curry powder

Kosher salt and freshly ground black pepper

Chopped chives for garnish

Place the eggs in a large pot of cold water and bring to a boil. Remove from the heat, cover, and let sit for 15 to 20 minutes. Drain carefully and let cool before peeling.

Slice the eggs in half lengthwise and remove the yolks, placing them in a large bowl. Place the egg white halves on a serving plate. Add the mayonnaise, lemon juice, and curry powder to the yolks. Use a fork to mash well and combine. Season with salt and pepper.

Using a spoon, fill the egg whites with generous spoonsful of the egg yolk mixture, dividing evenly. Sprinkle with the chives. Serve or cover and keep refrigerated for up to 1 day.

SERVES 12

QUICK SUMMERTIME GAZPACHO

4 large tomatoes, peeled and chopped

1½ cups [150 g] peeled and chopped English cucumber

1 red onion, peeled and chopped

½ cup [180 ml] extra-virgin olive oil

2 Tbsp white wine vinegar

1 tsp chopped garlic

Kosher salt and freshly ground black pepper

Tabasco sauce

Place the tomatoes, cucumber, onion, olive oil, vinegar, and garlic in a blender. Blend until puréed. Season with salt, pepper, and Tabasco. Chill in the refrigerator for 1 hour, or as long as overnight (this gazpacho is even better when served the next day). Serve chilled.

SERVES 4

15

GREEN BEAN, BELL PEPPER, JICAMA, AND TOMATO SALAD

1 lb [455 g] green beans, trimmed

1 yellow bell pepper, seeded and julienned

8 oz [225 g] jicama, peeled and julienned

15 cherry tomatoes, halved

DRESSING

1 tsp Dijon mustard

⅓ cup [75 ml] fresh lemon juice

1 tsp finely chopped chives

⅔ cup [165 ml] olive oil

Kosher salt and freshly ground black pepper

Bring a medium saucepan of water to a boil. Immerse the green beans in the boiling water and cook for 7 to 10 minutes, depending on their size. The beans should be slightly crisp. Drain and place in a bowl of ice water to stop the cooking. Drain well and place in a medium bowl. Add the bell pepper, jicama, and tomatoes.

TO MAKE THE DRESSING: In a small bowl, whisk together the mustard, lemon juice, and chives. Slowly add the olive oil, whisking until emulsified. Season with salt and pepper.

Add enough dressing to moisten the vegetables and thoroughly toss. Taste and adjust the seasonings. Transfer to a serving bowl and refrigerate for up to 1 day. Serve with the remaining dressing on the side.

SERVES 4 TO 6

CHILLED ASPARAGUS

RED PEPPER VINAIGRETTE
2 garlic cloves

1 shallot

3 Tbsp diced red bell pepper

2 Tbsp red wine vinegar

1 Tbsp balsamic vinegar

2 tsp fresh lemon juice

1 Tbsp mayonnaise

1 Tbsp finely chopped fresh basil

Kosher salt and freshly ground
black pepper

⅓ cup [75 ml] olive oil

2 lb [910 g] thin asparagus spears

2 Tbsp pine nuts

2 Tbsp diced red bell pepper

TO MAKE THE VINAIGRETTE: In a food processor, process the garlic, shallot, and 3 Tbsp bell pepper. Add both vinegars, the lemon juice, mayonnaise, and basil. Season with salt and pepper. Process until combined. With the motor running, slowly add the olive oil and process until blended. Taste and adjust the seasonings.

If the asparagus spears are thick, peel the stalks and cut off 1 in [2.5 cm] from the bottom. Bring a large skillet of salted water to a boil. Add the asparagus and cook for about 5 minutes, or just until tender. Remove and place on paper towels to drain.

Arrange the asparagus on a platter, cover, and refrigerate for about 2 hours. Place the pine nuts in a dry skillet over medium heat and toast until golden brown. Pour the vinaigrette evenly over the asparagus. Garnish with the remaining 2 Tbsp bell pepper and pine nuts, and serve.

SERVES 6 TO 8

GRILLED CORN

CHIPOTLE BUTTER
½ cup [115 g] butter, at room temperature

2 chipotle chiles in adobo, seeds removed and finely chopped

1 tsp minced garlic

½ tsp kosher salt

½ tsp freshly ground black pepper

6 ears corn, husked

TO MAKE THE CHIPOTLE BUTTER: In a small bowl, use a fork to mash together the butter, chipotles, garlic, salt, and pepper until just combined. Transfer the mixture to a 12-in [30.5-cm] piece of plastic wrap and use the wrap to roll the butter mixture into a log roughly the size of the original stick of butter. Place the butter in the refrigerator for up to 1 week.

Prepare enough coal for a medium-hot charcoal fire, or preheat your gas grill on medium-high for 10 minutes with the lid closed.
    Grill the corn for 10 to 12 minutes, turning frequently as the bottoms begin to turn a golden brown. Serve immediately, with the chipotle butter on the side.

SERVES 6

21

GRILLED SWEET POTATOES

4 sweet potatoes

½ cup [115 g] butter, melted

3 Tbsp honey

1 tsp ground cinnamon

¼ tsp freshly grated nutmeg

Kosher salt and freshly ground black pepper

Peel the sweet potatoes and cut them lengthwise into ¾-in- [2-cm-] thick slices. Bring 3 qt [2.8 L] water to a boil and add the sweet potato slices. Simmer until they are just starting to soften, about 12 minutes. Drain and let cool in a single layer on a large platter.

Combine the butter, honey, cinnamon, and nutmeg in a small saucepan and place over low heat, stirring to combine. Brush the potato slices on both sides with the butter mixture and season with salt and pepper.

Prepare enough coal for a medium-hot charcoal fire, or preheat your gas grill on medium-high for 10 minutes with the lid closed.

Grill the sweet potato slices for about 6 minutes, turning once, until they are soft through the middle and nicely browned. Serve immediately.

SERVES 4

23

GRILLED PIZZA

PIZZA DOUGH

4½ cups [570 g] unbleached high-gluten, bread, or all-purpose flour

1¾ tsp kosher salt

2 tsp instant yeast

¼ cup [60 ml] extra-virgin olive oil, plus more for drizzling

1¾ cups [420 ml] water

2 Tbsp extra-virgin olive oil

8 oz [225 g] white or cremini mushrooms, cut into ¼-in [6-mm] slices

One 115-g [4-oz] jar roasted red peppers, drained well and cut into ¼-in [6-mm] slices

1 Tbsp chopped fresh garlic

Kosher salt and freshly ground black pepper

2 cups [480 ml] pizza sauce

8 oz [225 g] fresh mozzarella, grated

170 g [6 oz] pepperoni, thinly sliced

Cornmeal for dusting

Semolina flour for dusting

TO MAKE THE DOUGH: Measure the flour, salt, and yeast into a large bowl. With a large wooden spoon, stir in the olive oil and water until all of the flour is absorbed. Continue stirring the dough vigorously into a smooth mass. (If the dough is too wet and doesn't come off the sides of the bowl, sprinkle in some more flour just until the dough clears the sides.)

CONT'D

Lightly flour the counter and knead the dough for 5 to 7 minutes until it is springy, elastic, and slightly sticky. Prepare a sheet pan by lining it with baking parchment and lightly oiling the parchment. Using a serrated knife, cut the dough into four equal pieces. Make sure your hands are dry, and then flour them. Lift each piece of dough and gently round it into a ball. Transfer the dough balls to the sheet pan, drizzle the dough with olive oil, and slip the pan into a clean plastic bag. Put the pan into the refrigerator overnight to rest the dough. It will keep for up to 2 days.

Remove the balls of pizza dough from the refrigerator. Clear a 2-ft [60-cm] square on the counter that you can use later for rolling out the dough. Place a large, heavy-bottomed skillet over medium-high heat. When the pan gets hot, add the 2 Tbsp olive oil, spreading it so it evenly coats the bottom of the pan. Add the mushrooms and cook, stirring regularly, until they soften, about 7 minutes. Add the roasted red peppers and garlic and cook for 1 minute more. Season with salt and pepper and transfer to a medium bowl. Set aside, or let cool, cover, and refrigerate for up to 24 hours.

Set the mushroom mixture, pizza sauce, grated cheese, and pepperoni on a table near the grill. Prepare enough coals for a hot charcoal fire, or preheat your gas grill on high for 10 minutes with the lid closed.

While the grill is getting hot, generously dust a metal pizza tray or the back of a sheet pan with cornmeal. Also generously dust your square of counter with semolina flour.

Using a rolling pin and working from the center, roll out one ball of the dough into a 12-in [30.5-cm] circle. Transfer the dough to the prepared pizza tray or the back of the sheet pan, making sure there is enough cornmeal to allow it to slide easily. Repeat with the other three pieces of dough, placing each one on a separate tray.

Bring one of the pizza trays to the grill and slide the dough onto the center of the grill grate. Grill for 2 to 3 minutes, or until golden brown. Turn over and immediately spoon a layer of sauce over the crust. Add one-quarter of the cheese, one-quarter of the mushroom mixture, then one-quarter of the pepperoni.

Continue grilling for 2 to 3 minutes more, until the crust is cooked through (this may happen before the cheese melts completely—but that's okay).

Bring the pizza tray close to the grill and slide the pizza on to it. Transfer to a large cutting board. Cut the pizza into six pieces, and transfer the slices to a large plate. Repeat for the remaining dough and toppings and serve.

MAKES FOUR 12-IN [30.5-CM] PIZZAS

GRILLED TEQUILA-LIME SHRIMP

MARINADE
¼ cup [60 ml] freshly squeezed lime juice

¼ cup [60 ml] tequila

2 garlic cloves, minced

2 shallots, finely chopped

2 tsp ground cumin

Kosher salt and freshly ground black pepper

½ cup [120 ml] olive oil

2 lb [910 g] large shrimp, unpeeled

Lime slices for garnish

1 bunch watercress, separated into sprigs, for garnish

TO MAKE THE MARINADE: In a small bowl, whisk together the lime juice, tequila, garlic, shallots, and cumin. Season with salt and pepper. Slowly add the olive oil, whisking until combined.

Thread 3 or 4 shrimp on each of four to six skewers. Lay the skewers in a shallow, nonaluminum dish. Pour the marinade over the shrimp and turn to coat evenly. Marinate in the refrigerator for at least 30 minutes, or up to 2 hours.

Prepare enough coals for a medium-hot charcoal fire, or preheat your gas grill on medium-high for 10 minutes with the lid closed. Remove the shrimp from the marinade, discarding the marinade. Grill the shrimp, turning them once with tongs, for about 4 minutes on each side, or until they are opaque. Remove the shrimp from the skewers and place on a serving plate. Garnish with the lime slices and watercress sprigs, and serve immediately.

SERVES 4 TO 6

GRILLED SNAPPER TACOS

ONION-CILANTRO TOPPING
1 sweet onion, finely chopped

1 bunch cilantro, finely chopped

¼ cup [60 ml] fresh lime juice

Kosher salt and freshly ground
black pepper

GUACAMOLE
2 ripe avocados

2 Roma tomatoes, seeded and cut
into ½-in [12-mm] dice

¼ cup [15 g] finely chopped red
onion

¼ cup [15 g] finely chopped
cilantro

¼ cup [60 ml] fresh lime juice,
plus more if needed

3 Tbsp finely chopped garlic

1 tsp kosher salt

Several dashes hot sauce

12 corn tortillas

2 lb [910 g] red snapper fillets

2 tsp chili powder

2 tsp paprika

2 tsp dried oregano

Kosher salt and freshly ground
black pepper

Olive oil for brushing

4 limes, quartered, for serving

Hot sauce for serving

CONT'D

TO MAKE THE ONION-CILANTRO TOPPING: In a medium bowl, mix together the chopped onion, cilantro, and lime juice. Season with salt and pepper. Set aside, or cover and refrigerate for up to 4 hours.

TO MAKE THE GUACAMOLE: Cut each avocado in half lengthwise, remove the pit, and scoop out the meat into a mixing bowl. Mash the avocados with a potato masher or the back of a fork. Add the tomatoes, onion, cilantro, lime juice, garlic, salt, and hot sauce and mix together. Taste and adjust the seasonings as necessary.

Wrap the tortillas in aluminum foil, in three packages of four tortillas each. Place the tortilla packages in the oven and set it at 250°F [120°C]. Warm for up to 30 minutes.

Prepare enough coals for a hot charcoal fire, or preheat your gas grill on high for 10 minutes with the lid closed.

Season the tops of the snapper fillets with the chili powder, paprika, oregano, and a sprinkling of salt and pepper. Liberally brush the skin side of each snapper fillet with olive oil. Place the fillets on the grate, skin-side down, and grill for 4 minutes, until the skin is golden brown and a crust has formed. Brush the tops of the fillets again with oil, turn, and grill for 4 to 5 minutes more, until the center is just cooked through.

Transfer the snapper fillets to a cutting board, and cut them into quarters. Serve the fish with the warm tortillas, onion-cilantro mixture, guacamole, limes, and hot sauce and let people assemble their own tacos.

SERVES 6 TO 12

GRILLED STRIPED BASS

TOMATO AND CORN SALSA

1 lb [455 g] cherry tomatoes, halved

1 small red onion, halved lengthwise, and cut into thin slices

One 6-oz [170-g] can corn kernels packed in water, drained well

One 4-oz [115-g] jar roasted red peppers, drained well and cut into medium dice

¼ cup [15 g] coarsely chopped flat-leaf parsley

¼ cup [15 g] coarsely chopped fresh basil leaves

2 Tbsp finely chopped fresh mint

2½ Tbsp fresh lemon juice

¼ cup [60 ml] extra virgin olive oil

Freshly ground black pepper

Four 6-oz [170-g] striped bass fillets

Kosher salt and freshly ground black pepper

Olive oil for brushing

TO MAKE THE SALSA: In a medium bowl, combine the tomatoes, onion, corn, roasted red peppers, parsley, basil, mint, lemon juice, and olive oil. Season with pepper, toss gently, and set aside.

Prepare enough coals for a hot charcoal fire, or preheat your gas grill on high for 10 minutes with the lid closed. Season both sides of the bass with salt and pepper. Liberally brush the skin side of the fillets with olive oil. Place the fillets on the grate, skin-side down, and grill for 4 minutes, until the skin is golden brown and a crust has formed. Brush the fillets again with oil, turn, and grill for 3 to 4 minutes more, until they are just cooked through.

Transfer the bass to individual plates, top with the salsa, and serve.

SERVES 4

GRILLED SALMON

MANGO SALSA
3 Tbsp [45 ml] freshly squeezed lime juice

½ cup [30 g] chopped cilantro

1 small red onion, finely chopped

1 mango, coarsely chopped

1 red bell pepper, stemmed, seeded, and finely chopped

½ tsp chili powder

½ tsp kosher salt

Dash of hot sauce

Four 6-oz [170-g] salmon fillets

Extra-virgin olive oil for brushing

TO MAKE THE SALSA: In a medium bowl, combine the lime juice, cilantro, red onion, mango, bell pepper, chili powder, salt, and hot sauce. Toss gently and set aside.

Prepare enough coals for a hot charcoal fire, or preheat your gas grill on high for 10 minutes with the lid closed. Liberally brush the skin side of the fillets with olive oil. Place the salmon fillets on the grate, skin-side down, and grill for 5 minutes, until the skin is golden brown and a crust has formed. Brush the top of the fillets again with oil, turn, and grill for 4 to 5 minutes more, until the center is just cooked through.

Transfer the salmon to individual plates, top with the salsa, and serve.

SERVES 4

GRILLED CHICKEN

CHIMICHURRI SAUCE
10 whole, peeled garlic cloves

1 bunch flat-leaf parsley

¼ cup [60 ml] olive oil

¼ cup [60 ml] balsamic vinegar

¼ cup [60 ml] water

¾ tsp dried oregano

¾ tsp dried basil

¼ tsp red pepper flakes

Kosher salt and freshly ground black pepper

6 skin-on, boneless chicken breast halves

TO MAKE THE SAUCE: In a food processor, purée the garlic. Strip the parsley leaves from the stems and process. Add the olive oil, vinegar, water, oregano, basil, and red pepper flakes. Process until blended. Season with salt and pepper.

Place each chicken breast half between two pieces of plastic wrap. Using a meat mallet, pound to an even thickness of about 1½ in [4 cm]. Place the chicken breasts in a large resealable plastic bag. Add 3 Tbsp of the sauce. Seal the bag and marinate in the refrigerator for at least 30 minutes, or up to 4 hours, turning occasionally.

Prepare enough coals for a hot charcoal fire, or preheat your gas grill on high for 10 minutes with the lid closed. Discard the marinade and grill the chicken for 7 to 10 minutes on each side, or until opaque throughout. Serve with the sauce on the side.

SERVES 4 TO 6

HONEY-GLAZED SPARERIBS

HONEY GLAZE

⅔ cup [230 g] honey

½ cup [120 ml] freshly squeezed orange juice

¼ cup [60 ml] freshly squeezed lemon juice

3 Tbsp soy sauce

2 Tbsp Dijon-style mustard

1 Tbsp sesame oil

1 tsp curry powder

1 tsp ground ginger

BRAISING LIQUID

½ cup [120 ml] white wine

½ cup [120 ml] soy sauce

1 bunch scallions, green parts only, finely chopped

3 Tbsp finely chopped fresh ginger

8 garlic cloves, coarsely chopped

6 Tbsp [75 g] firmly packed light brown sugar

1 Tbsp Chinese five-spice power

Pinch of cayenne pepper

3 to 4 lb [1.4 to 1.8 kg] spareribs, cut into sections of ribs

TO MAKE THE GLAZE: In a medium bowl, stir together the honey, orange juice, lemon juice, soy sauce, mustard, sesame oil, curry powder, and ground ginger. Set aside until ready to use, or refrigerate, covered, for up to 1 week. Let the glaze come to room temperature before using.

CONT'D

TO MAKE THE BRAISING LIQUID: In a large bowl, combine the wine, soy sauce, scallions, fresh ginger, garlic, brown sugar, five-spice powder, and cayenne.

Place the ribs in the bowl with the braising liquid, tossing them gently so they are all coated evenly.

Preheat the oven to 350°F [180°C]. Transfer the ribs and liquid to a baking pan, cover with foil, and bake in the center of the oven for 1 hour. Let the ribs cool, then transfer them to a container or platter and refrigerate for up to 2 days.

Prepare enough coals for a medium-hot charcoal fire, or preheat your gas grill on medium-high for 10 minutes with the lid closed. Grill the ribs until they are heated through, about 15 minutes, turning and mopping them several times with the Honey Glaze so they are nicely coated. Serve immediately with lots of napkins.

SERVES 4

GRILLED LAMB CHOPS
WITH CILANTRO-MINT SAUCE

CILANTRO-MINT SAUCE
2 tsp minced fresh ginger

¼ cup [15 g] fresh mint leaves

¼ cup [15 g] fresh cilantro leaves

1 Tbsp honey

¼ cup [60 ml] rice vinegar

½ cup [120 ml] canola oil

Kosher salt and freshly ground black pepper

8 rib lamb chops, no more than ¾ in [2 cm] thick

TO MAKE THE SAUCE: In a food processor, combine the ginger, mint, cilantro, honey, vinegar, and canola oil. Process until blended and smooth. Season with salt and pepper.

Place the lamb chops in a large resealable plastic bag. Add ¼ cup [60 ml] of the sauce. Seal the bag and marinate in the refrigerator for at least 30 minutes, or up to 4 hours, turning the bag once or twice.

Prepare enough coals for a medium-hot charcoal fire, or preheat your gas grill on medium-high for 10 minutes with the lid closed. Discard the marinade and grill the lamb chops for 5 to 7 minutes, or until medium-rare (registers 120°F [50°C] on an instant-read meat thermometer inserted in the thickest part of the chop). Serve the chops with the sauce on the side.

SERVES 4

45

FOOLPROOF BURGERS

1½ lb [680 g] ground round

Kosher salt

4 classic hamburger buns

Condiments of your choice
for serving

Shape the meat into four 6-oz [170-g] burgers, each about ¾ in [2 cm] thick and 4 in [10 cm] across.

Prepare enough coals for a hot charcoal fire, or preheat your gas grill on high for 10 minutes with the lid closed. Sprinkle the burgers with salt and grill them for 8 to 9 minutes, turning once, until they are medium-rare. Transfer each burger to a bun. Add condiments and serve.

SERVES 4

NECTARINE TART

TART SHELL

1½ cups [185 g] all-purpose flour

⅛ tsp salt

¾ cup [170 g] cold unsalted butter

1 to 3 Tbsp ice water

FILLING

2½ lb [1.2 kg] nectarines, peels left on, halved, pitted, and cut into ½-in [12-mm] slices

½ cup [100 g] sugar

2 Tbsp cornstarch

1 tsp kosher salt

2 tsp all-purpose flour

1 Tbsp unsalted chilled butter, cubed

TO MAKE THE TART SHELL: Combine the flour and salt in a large mixing bowl or food processor. Cut the butter into small pieces and work into the flour, using a pastry cutter or pulsing in the food processor. When the dough resembles a course meal, add the ice water, 1 Tbsp at a time, just until the dough sticks together. Pat the dough into a flattened ball, wrap with plastic wrap, and refrigerate for 15 to 30 minutes.

CONT'D

Remove the dough and as soon as it is pliable, roll it out on a lightly floured surface into a circle approximately $\frac{1}{8}$ in [4 mm] thick and at least 13 in [33 cm] in diameter. (You may have extra dough.) Gently place the rolled dough into an 11-in [28-cm] tart pan with a removable bottom so that it covers the bottom and sides completely. (Patch any small holes or tears by pressing on extra pieces of rolled dough glued on with a dab of ice water.) To remove the dough hanging over the edges of the tart pan, use a knife or take a rolling pin and roll it over the rim of the pan.

Cover the tart shell with plastic wrap and freeze for at least 1 hour (or up to 1 month). Do not defrost the tart shell before filling.

TO MAKE THE FILLING: Place the nectarines in a large bowl. Combine the sugar, cornstarch, and salt in another bowl, and mix well. Add the sugar mixture to the nectarines and gently combine.

Arrange an oven rack on the lowest level of the oven and preheat to 375°F [190°C]. Sprinkle the flour onto the bottom of the frozen tart shell, spreading it around to thinly cover the entire bottom. (This will help prevent a soggy bottom crust.) Put the nectarine filling into the shell and arrange the nectarines so that as many as possible are on the bottom, rather than stacked; sprinkle the cubed butter over the nectarines.

Bake for approximately 1 hour, or until the crust is golden brown and the nectarines are tender and a little brown or the edges have caramelized. (The long baking time gives the nectarines an intense flavor and helps assure that they will not be too juicy.) Let cool to room temperature, then slice and serve.

SERVES 8 TO 10

ENGLISH BERRY SUMMER PUDDING

2 lb [910 g] fresh mixed berries (any combination of raspberries, blackberries, strawberries, or blueberries)

½ cup [100 g] sugar

¼ cup [60 ml] water

1 to 2 Tbsp freshly squeezed lemon juice

8 to 12 slices (approximately ¼ in [6 mm] thick) stale, good-quality bread, such as challah

2 cups [480 ml] heavy cream

If using strawberries, trim and chop into pieces. Place the fruit, sugar, water, and lemon juice in a large saucepan and bring to a boil. Lower to a simmer and cook until the sugar has dissolved and the fruit begins to get juicy, 3 to 5 minutes. Stir gently. The idea is not to cook the fruit as much as to get the berries to release their juices. Allow the mixture to cool.

Cut off the crust from the bread. In a large serving bowl, put a layer of the fruit and then top it with a layer of bread slices, being sure the bread covers the entire surface of the fruit. Continue to layer the fruit and bread, ending with the fruit. Cover the top with plastic wrap, weigh it down with something (such as a bag of rice or beans) to help the bread absorb all of the juices, and refrigerate for at least 1 day, or up to 2 days.

To serve, use a large spoon to scoop into serving bowls, being sure to get several layers of the bread and berries. Pour a few spoonsful of cream over each serving.

SERVES 6

HONEY-GINGER LEMONADE

4 cups [960 ml] water

1½ cups [510 g] honey

1 cup [200 g] sugar

1 cup [120 g] finely chopped fresh ginger

3 cups [720 ml] freshly squeezed lemon juice

Bring 2 cups [480 ml] of the water plus the honey, sugar, and ginger to a boil in a medium saucepan. Let simmer for a couple of minutes until the sugar and honey are dissolved. Remove from the heat. Let stand for 20 to 30 minutes. Strain and combine with the lemon juice in a large pitcher. Let cool completely. Add the remaining 2 cups [480 ml] water. The lemonade should be tart-sweet at this point. (Add more water to taste or plan to serve over lots of ice, taking into consideration that some of it will melt and dilute the lemonade.) Chill until ready to serve.

SERVES 8

WATERMELON-LIME AGUA FRESCA

6 cups [900 g] chunked seedless watermelon

½ cup [120 ml] water

3 Tbsp sugar

¼ cup [60 ml] freshly squeezed lime juice, plus lime wedges for garnish

Kosher salt

Ice cubes for serving

Place the watermelon chunks in a blender and purée. In a small pan over medium heat, heat the water and add the sugar, stirring until the sugar dissolves. Remove from the heat and let cool completely. Pour the watermelon purée into a pitcher. Stir in the lime juice, a pinch of salt, and the sugar syrup to taste. Chill until ready to serve. Serve over ice with the lime wedges.

SERVES 4

PRICKLY AGAVE

Bar sugar and bar salt for rimming glasses

1½ oz [45 ml] good-quality silver tequila

1 oz [30 ml] Tuaca

2 oz [60 ml] prickly pear juice

1 oz [30 ml] freshly squeezed lime juice, plus thinly sliced lime wedge for garnish

Ice cubes for shaking

Chill a margarita or cocktail glass, then dip the rim once in the sugar and once in the salt to coat well.

Combine the tequila, Tuaca, prickly pear juice, and lime juice in a shaker with ice and shake vigorously. Strain into the prepared glass. Float the lime wedge on top of the drink. Repeat for as many drinks as you wish to serve.

SERVES 1

SOUTH SEAS SANGRIA

1 pineapple, peeled, cored, and sliced

2 mangoes, peeled, pitted, and sliced

1 star fruit, sliced

½ cantaloupe, cubed

2 nectarines, pitted and sliced

1 blood orange or tangerine, quartered and sliced

1 lemon, quartered and sliced

20 whole cloves

2 oz [60ml] Grand Marnier

2 oz [60 ml] brandy

3 Tbsp superfine sugar

Two 750-ml bottles rosé wine, such as white rioja or a pinot grigio

Ice cubes for serving

In a large (at least 2-qt [2-L]) glass pitcher, combine the pineapple, mangoes, star fruit, cantaloupe, nectarines, blood orange, lemon, cloves, Grand Marnier, brandy, and sugar and stir until the sugar is dissolved. Slowly pour in the wine, stirring gently. Cover and refrigerate for at least 2 hours, or as long as overnight, to chill.

When ready to serve, fill highball glasses or wine goblets with ice cubes, and strain the sangria over the ice.

SERVES 6 TO 8

MOJITOS

1 cup [60 g] fresh mint leaves, plus more for garnish

¾ cup [180 ml] light rum

½ cup [120 ml] freshly squeezed lemon juice

¼ cup [60 ml] freshly squeezed lime juice

¼ cup [50 g] sugar

1⅓ cups [315 ml] soda water

Ice cubes for serving

In the bottom of a pitcher, crush the mint leaves with the back of a long-handled wooden spoon. Add the rum, lemon juice, lime juice, and sugar and mix together.

Just before serving add the soda water. Serve over ice, garnished with a mint leaf.

SERVES 4